SUICIDE

TROUBLED

SOCIETY

SUICIDE

Leslie McGuire

The Rourke Corporation, Inc.

The Rourke Corporation, Inc.
P.O. Box 3328, Vero Beach, FL 32964

McGuire, Leslie.
    Suicide / by Leslie McGuire.
        p. cm. — (Troubled society)
    Includes bibliographical references.
    Summary: Examines the historic and legal views of suicide, the reasons that people trun to suicide, and how suicide may be prevented.
    ISBN 0-86593-069-4
        1. Teenagers—United States—Suicidal behavior—Juvenile literature. 2. Suicide—United States—Prevention—Juvenile literature. [1. Suicide.] I. Title. II. Series.
HV6546.M39 1990   90-35678
362.2'8'09—dc20   CIP
                                                                                          AC

Series Editor: Gregory Lee
Editors: Elizabeth Sirimarco, Marguerite Aronowitz
Book design and production: The Creative Spark,
    Capistrano Beach, CA
Cover photograph: Larry Mulvehill, Science Source/Photo Researchers, Inc.

SUICIDE

Contents

YOUNG PEOPLE AND SUICIDE

Sixteen-year-old Andrea was told to stop and talk to her math teacher after class. She knew what was coming because her grades had been slipping in the last few months. But when her teacher told her that she was planning to call Andrea's parents in for a conference, Andrea was filled with despair.

She didn't go to her next class. Instead, Andrea went to the girls room, and using her nail file, she slashed her wrists. She was found a half hour later by another student and taken to the hospital.

Andrea didn't die, but she wanted to.

Andrea is one of many teenagers in the United States and worldwide, who feels that the pressures of life make it unliveable. Her case isn't that unusual.

For the person thinking about suicide, life can be a very lonely experience.

"I just couldn't talk to my mother and father," Andrea said. "It's not that they did anything wrong, but they want me to be perfect. I guess I'm just not perfect enough."

Andrea's parents are a middle class suburban couple who both work hard to maintain a nice house, two cars, and their status as high achievers. They wanted Andrea to fit into their lifestyle and be an example of what good parents they were.

"When I tried to tell them I was unhappy, they would close their faces," Andrea said. "I could see what they were thinking. 'I don't have time for this right now. Just don't make any waves right now.

Do the right thing, or what will our friends think?'"

A year before Andrea's attempt to kill herself, her parents started having problems of their own. Andrea's mother began a new and very demanding job. Andrea's father was resentful of his wife's position and the reduced amount of time she spent with her family. There were fights.

In addition, Andrea's boyfriend of six months told her he wanted to date other girls. She begged him not to, then finally accepted the situation. But she had seen him several times with new girlfriends, and was feeling very rejected. She was also feeling humiliated in front of what few friends she had.

"It wasn't like the math grade was the big thing," Andrea said. "It was just everything coming all at once. There was nobody to talk to, nobody who understood."

Andrea was suffering from feelings of great loneliness and loss. Her parents were not available to her because they were so wrapped up in themselves. She was under tremendous pressure to do as well or better than they did. She was feeling like another material possession.

"I know what they thought," she said.

"We have an expensive house. We drive expensive cars. Our daughter is just like everything else we have—the best."

"I couldn't stand the thought of not being what they wanted."

When Andrea's boyfriend left her, her self-esteem was attacked. She believed she wasn't good enough for him, either. She felt her parents would have preferred another, more perfect daughter, and that her boyfriend wanted another, better girlfriend.

Up until the time her math teacher spoke to her, Andrea managed to keep her fears under control. But knowing that her parents would be brought into school and told of her bad grades brought Andrea's despair to a head. So she tried to take her own life.

Fortunately, Andrea was found before it was too late. Her parents went into therapy with her, and many of their problems were resolved. Now, three years later, Andrea is doing well, and feels she has more control over her life.

Being Young Is Not Easy

Growing up is not as easy as many children are told. People often say, "Aren't you lucky to be a child? One of these days you'll look back on these years and say they were the happiest of your life. No responsibilities, no worries."

That is a very simplistic thing to tell a young person. It ignores very real problems. The response to such a remark is often, "If this is the good part, then I'd rather not deal with the rest!"

When young people enter adolescence, there are very big changes in their lives, their bodies, how the world views them, and how they view the world. They are expected to act like adults, yet they are often still treated like children. Their bodies begin to look and feel different. They have new feelings and new thoughts. Friends, teachers, parents, sisters and brothers all start treating young people differently.

Teenagers have to face all of these challenges at once. It is a very confusing time in their lives. How should they deal with sex, drugs, career, family problems, peer group pressure? Some handle these problems and challenges well. Some don't. Some resolve all the important questions, and some resolve only a few. All teenagers know they need to come to grips with these problems. Just like anybody else, they want life to be smoother and more manageable. Unfortunately, some teenagers feel the problems are much too hard for them. They choose to make their problems go away in the most final and self-destructive way: suicide.

Suicide

Teenagers who think about suicide are doubly burdened. Not only are they feeling suicidal, they also feel they can't talk about it to anyone. There is a taboo against discussing suicide. Some adults think that if you talk to young people about suicide, you will "put ideas in their heads." Some people feel that it is morally wrong, and therefore not a topic for discussion. Other people feel that if a young person starts talking about taking his or her own life, all they are doing is saying, "You are a bad parent, and this is how I'm going to get even with you."

Bad parents are not necessarily the cause of suicide in young people. However, family problems and lack of communication are often very serious contributing factors.

Remember Andrea? Her parents weren't bad people. They didn't abuse her. But they had very high expectations of her. That, added to their inability to communicate with her, put Andrea in a tough position. Perhaps her boyfriend or her friends could have helped, but by the time her math teacher talked to her, Andrea had already begun a process of withdrawal.

Few young people who attempt or succeed in committing suicide really want to die. Their desire to live is as strong as their desire to die. They are desperately reaching out for help. But in spite of all human beings' powerful desire to live, suicide among young people is the third most common cause of death between the ages of 15 and 19. The first two are accidents and homicide (murder). In the college years, it is the second most common cause of death. Suicide is a major national problem.

Let's examine the other two causes of death among young people. Both accidents and homicide can also be seen as self-destructive behavior. It is possible that many car accidents that are reported as being the result of drunk or reckless driving could, in fact, have been suicides. Without a note or some other evidence, who really knows what was going on in that teenage driver's head before they crashed into a tree?

Homicide, too, might be the result of an open invitation to get killed. After all, deliberately putting yourself in the path of violence is certainly self-destructive behavior. But this is not to suggest that all victims are guilty. For example, if you are a gang member and you engage in a street battle where everyone is armed with guns or knives, a powerful possibility exists that you will die. This could be a deliberately self-destructive act, but the police report on your death would read "homicide," not "suicide."

In the musical *West Side Story*, a teenager is faced with the loss of his girlfriend and decides he doesn't want to live anymore. He goes into the rival gang's territory without any protection and says to the gang leader, "Come and get me." The gang does exactly what the young man wants—they kill him.

Other Causes

There are also other, slower deaths that young people choose. Drugs and alcohol are often connected with suicides. They may not cause the suicide, but drug and alcohol abuse is a symptom of the deep loneliness and fear that young people can feel. Both drugs and alcohol are used to control and suppress the level of pain they feel.

Suicide and the use of drugs and alcohol point to some common problems among young people: depression, lack of self-esteem, inability to deal with problems, feeling unloved by those who are important, and a deep sense of loss. If a young person is feeling unloved and unwanted, who cares what he does with his mind or his body?

Ted

Ted's father had lost several jobs. His mother just had a new baby. Ted had never done that well in school, but at least he was keeping his head above water. He had always felt slightly embarrassed by his parents. They lived on the edges of an affluent neighborhood, and he didn't have any friends at school.

"Once the baby came, all hell broke loose at

SUICIDE STATISTICS

• Among females, the typical suicide attempter is a single woman under age 25, often as young as 15.

• A recent study suggests that up to 47 percent of suicides may be the result of a major illness or alcoholism.

• Among males, the typical suicide attempter is a white male between the ages of 20 and 24.

• Since the mid-1950s suicide among the 15- to 24-year-old population increased more than 200 percent.

• The rate of completed suicides among the 10- to 14-year-old age group is an alarming 1.1 per 100,000 people.

home," he said. "My mother stopped working, my father drank a lot, and they always fought about money. They fought about the baby, too. It was like they didn't want either of us. But we didn't ask to be born."

Ted was feeling frustrated, lonely and angry. There was no one he could express his anger to, no one to hear his cries for help. But the whole family needed help, and so his needs were never even acknowledged. The new baby made things even worse for him. The baby's needs were taken care of, but those needs were easy to identify and satisfy: food, warmth, diaper change. Ted's needs were more adult and complex. His parents weren't able to deal with their own frustrations, much less his.

Ted started looking around for something that would "stop the pain." He saw that drugs and alcohol were the easiest way to medicate himself. At that point, Ted didn't literally want to kill himself, he just didn't want to feel so much pain. That was when his downward spiral began. Ted's body became weakened by the abuse. He was setting himself up for an accidental overdose, or even death. When he was old enough to drive, Ted got another lethal weapon to abuse—a driver's license.

One night after a particularly nasty argument with his father, Ted grabbed his mother's car keys and stormed out of the house. He raced the engine and was gone. There was a sharp turn ahead in the road. Ted was going too fast. The car jumped the guard rail, plunged over an embankment, and burst into flames. Perhaps Ted drove recklessly because of all the adrenaline he was feeling from the argument. Certainly he was angry. He may have been saying, "I'll show them. They'll be sorry."

Even though Ted's death was listed as an accident, everything leading up to the accident could be considered suicidal behavior.

There are so many single-driver automobile deaths that experts are beginning to call them *auto-*

cides. They seem to be much more self-destructive than accidents occurring during rain storms or traffic jams.

All young people are under great pressure during puberty. Adolescence is a time of emotional stress fed by physical and chemical changes in their bodies. Teenagers want the right to make adult decisions, yet they are still emotionally very fragile.

Additionally, the family structure has changed. More families are isolated from their relatives. The *extended family* (where several generations live closely together) no longer exists. Internal supports that used to keep children nurtured and attached to their families for a greater part of their lives are eroding away in our fast-forward society.

Parents are also under greater financial stress. More than 70 percent of all women work outside the home. When young people enter their most stressful period, it can seem as if no one has the time or energy to help them build their sliding self-esteem. When school or peers become a problem, there is often no one around to listen or talk to them about their feelings of isolation and loneliness.

The worst part, however, seems to be that teenagers don't realize that these troubled feelings will eventually go away.

TWO

An Age-Old Problem

Suicide is a human problem. But there are many different reactions to suicide by different cultures in the world. There have been many different attitudes toward taking your own life throughout history. Various cultures in some periods of history accepted suicide as a logical response to social or personal problems. Cultures such as our own do not accept suicide on any level.

Suicide as a behavior has probably always been around, but there is no prehistoric record to confirm this. The first written account of a suicide is from an ancient Egyptian manuscript from about 4,000 years ago. Much of the manuscript is missing, so there are different views on what the writer's state of mind was when he wrote it. One view is that he was tired of life. He was trying to convince his soul to follow him into the afterlife so he could have a wonderful eternity. Other historians think that suicide had nothing to do with the manuscript at all. The work merely describes two different attitudes toward death.

The early Greeks accepted some suicides, but this was only to escape real suffering, and only after all the alternatives had been considered. The later Greeks accepted suicide only to avoid disgrace. Otherwise, taking one's own life was considered a shameful act.

The Romans thought suicide was acceptable in the case of incurable illness or the extreme difficulties of old age. Any other reason was against Roman law. Suicide was especially illegal if the person who took his life, or attempted to take his life, was a slave or a soldier. This was because the state or the master was the one who controlled that person's life. So destroying one's self meant destroying someone else's property. Oddly enough, the

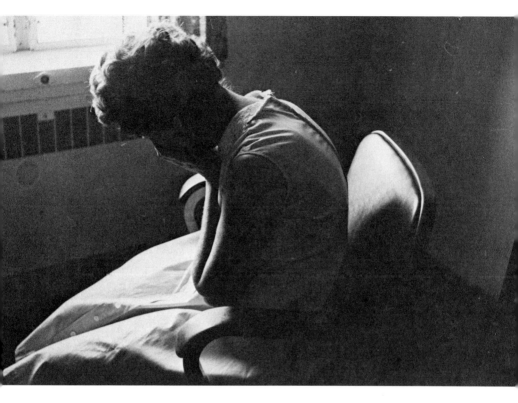

Depression can lead to a vicious cycle of withdrawal from others, increasing feelings of loneliness, which in turn can increase one's depression.

death penalty was given to anyone who attempted suicide and failed!

Suicide as a form of martyrdom was acceptable in the Judeo-Christian and Islamic countries. For example, when the fortress of Masada was under siege by the Romans in A.D. 73, one thousand Jewish men, women and children killed themselves rather than face slavery under the Romans. The Islamic religion promises that anyone who dies while killing an enemy of God will go directly to paradise regardless of their past mistakes.

Eskimos once practiced suicide out of social need.

In the United
States, many
teenagers take
their own
lives each year.

If there were too little food to feed the
rest of the group, the elderly would go
out on the ice flows. They ate nothing
and exposed themselves to the extreme
cold until death came.

Suicide was once the only honor-

able way for a Japanese warrior to deal with disgrace. The preferred method was to disembowel oneself with a ceremonial sword. This practice was called *hara-kiri*. Suicide was not considered a crime, but a way of wiping out a crime. If you took your own life, you were then innocent, and could keep the full respect of one's

Young people are not the only ones who think about suicide. Many seniors experience health problems, loneliness after the death of a spouse, and financial difficulties that often lead to despair.

family and society. During World War II, thousands of Japanese fighter pilots killed themselves by flying their planes directly into the warships of their enemies. They were called *kamikaze* pilots, and their self-inflicted deaths were considered heroic by the Japanese.

Among Native American Indians there were also different attitudes toward suicide. The Kwakiutl of the Pacific Northwest were very ashamed of making mistakes or bad decisions. If someone, for example, lost at gambling and had his property taken away, he could always avoid permanent shame by killing himself. This often happened.

Among the Pueblos, however, suicide was thought too violent even to be considered. The Pueblos also had such a low incidence of homicide that they can barely remember such things in their oral history.

The Christian attitude toward suicide has also changed. The Bible does not specifically forbid suicide. In fact, in early Christian philosophy there was a lot of enthusiasm for martyred holy men and women. Martyrs are not considered to be suicides by Christians. These people chose death rather than give up their faith. It was also considered acceptable to kill yourself to protect your honor or virginity.

In wasn't until A.D. 452 that the Roman Catholic Church forbid suicide of any kind. The Council of Arles said, "whoever kills himself kills an innocent person. Therefore it is homicide." The belief of this time was that people owed their lives to God, so only God could decide how and when those lives would end.

From the Middle Ages until recently, punishment for suicide included poor treatment or dismemberment of the body, and refusal by the church to bury the person in holy ground.

In England, if someone committed suicide, their property was taken from them and their surviving heirs by the government. Attempted suicide was still considered a felony and punishable by law until 1961. In the United States personal property was never taken as punishment for suicide: however, suicide was considered illegal in New York State until 1919.

Suicide Laws Today

Suicide is still considered a crime in nine states, and some states define it as a misdemeanor. Eighteen states have no laws forbidding suicide, but New York, Missouri, Wisconsin and California laws say that help-

A minister, priest or rabbi can sometimes provide support to an individual that is going through a difficult time.

ing someone commit suicide is a criminal offense.

There can be, however, economic punishment. Insurance companies may refuse to pay death benefits to survivors in the case of suicide.

Public opinion is generally very much against suicide. This is one reason that accurate statistics about suicide are hard to come by. Many deaths may, in fact, be suicides. But because of the embarrassment felt by loved ones and families, a suicide is often reported as an accident of some kind.

Sometimes it is difficult to define what constitutes a suicide. There are still some cases where opinion is in favor of someone who purposely chooses death. For example, is a soldier who refuses to retreat or surrender and is killed committing suicide? This sort of patriotic death is considered acceptable. Religious martyrs who choose to die rather than give up their faith have often been applauded and respected. People who choose death rather than reveal secrets under torture are also thought to be heroes and patriots.

As we have seen, throughout history and in every culture there have been many different ways of looking at suicide. In the United States, there doesn't seem to be any one universal reaction to the taking of one's own life. Instead, there seems to be a veil of secrecy about it. No one wants to talk about it. No one wants to confront the reasons for it. As a result, many young people who could benefit from open communication on the subject and get help, are lost in the maze of their own loneliness and despair.

It has been said that suicide is a permanent solution to a temporary problem. It is like killing a fly with an atom bomb. The real issue is that suicide is far too dramatic a solution to an ongoing personal problem. That problem is one of communication. If families would talk to each other, if students could talk to their teachers, if friends could listen to one another, the problem of suicide in young people would have some hope of being resolved.
being resolved.

SOCIAL AND EMOTIONAL CAUSES OF SUICIDE

Whenever anyone commits suicide, the first question people ask is, "Why?" Obviously the person was upset. But lots of people get upset. Only a few of them kill themselves. What is the difference between the people who choose to live and the people who choose to die?

Social Causes

It was once believed that people who killed themselves were possessed by demons. In the 16th and 17th centuries, thinkers such as John Donne and Thomas Hobbes felt the question of suicide should really be a question of people's rights. Whether or not a person chooses to live or die, they said, was a decision to be made by that person alone. Since science took a dim view of demons as the cause for things, it needed to look at the reasons why people made certain choices for their lives.

Emotional problems are not the only cause of suicide. Suicide can result from mental illness as well.

It wasn't until the 19th century that sociologists and psychologists made some major breakthroughs on the causes of suicide. They studied individual cases. They decided that instead of one cause, there were many. A suicidal person didn't have just one problem. Often there were things about the society in which that person lived that made suicide more acceptable.

A tendency to commit suicide is not inherited the way blue eyes or brown hair might be. It doesn't run in certain families, either. Suicide does not occur more often among people who are mentally ill. Even though suicidal

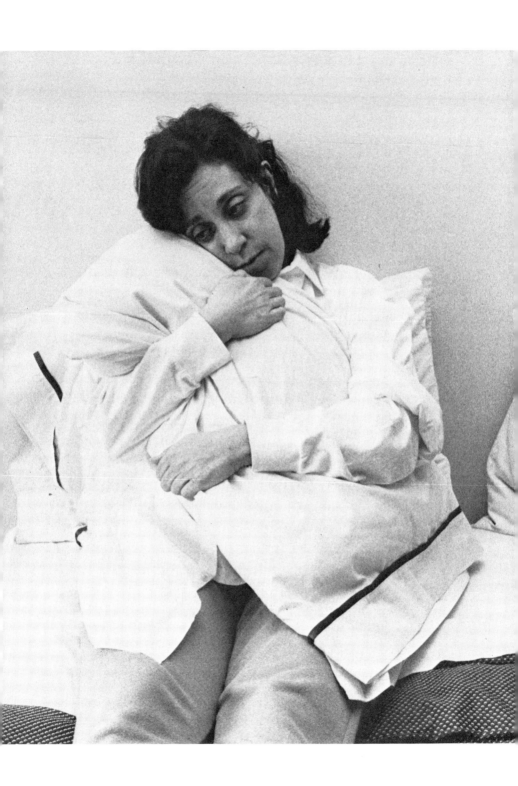

people are clearly unhappy, being unhappy doesn't mean a person is mentally ill.

If someone once tried to kill himself or herself, it doesn't follow that they will live with a life-long tendency to do it again. Usually, wanting to kill yourself is a temporary desire. Once the problem has been faced and resolved, most people never become seriously suicidal again. This does not mean, however, that they can never suffer a relapse of depression.

Suicide has nothing to do with gender or social stature. It is not prevented by being rich. It also has nothing to do with the phases of the moon, the position of the stars, or any other cosmic factor.

Some countries do have higher suicide rates than others. Experts looked for a common thread, but only came up with a lot of theories. One is that Catholic countries have fewer suicides because Catholicism forbids suicide. Another is that developed countries have a higher suicide rate than underdeveloped countries, but this has not been supported by statistics.

In underdeveloped nations, two factors that discourage suicide are at work. First, children stay home with their families longer. In addition, people in underdeveloped nations desperately want to raise their standard of living. They work hard. That desire may give added direction to people's lives, and psychologists feel that having a main goal in life acts as a suicide preventive.

There are other social reasons why young people kill themselves. Students often become very depressed when they discover the gap between their own idealism and the way the rest of the world behaves. It is hard to balance out society's love of material wealth

Teenagers, perhaps more than any other age group, rely strongly on the approval of others for their self-esteem.

with our search for spiritual happiness.

Sometimes a single dramatic event that threatens a young person's happiness or even the fate of a nation will trigger a number of suicides. The death of a wonderful leader, or the death of a young person's idol often leads to feelings of despair and hopelessness.

In some countries, society places strong demands on young people to show—at the very least—competence, and—at the most—excellence. For example, Japan has an extremely high suicide rate among young people around exam time. At the end of high school there is an exam that can either make or break a young person's career. Without high grades, there is a tremendous loss of economic power as well as respect from the family and the community. The Japanese call it "Examination Hell," and many teenagers, fearing disgrace, kill themselves instead of facing the possible humiliation of doing poorly.

Some social groups in the United States have very strong family ties. For example, the role of the family among Irish- and Italian-Americans helps keep their suicide rate down. In the country of Denmark, however, people are more tolerant of suicide. Denmark is known for its social openness toward personal freedoms. Danish law does not forbid taking one's own life. This cultural attitude may help make their suicide rate higher.

Emotional Causes

The most important causes of suicide are emotional. Almost all suicidal behavior comes from a sense of isolation combined with overwhelming emotional distress. Young people who try to kill themselves usually have trouble developing relationships or keeping them. They are often described as "loners."

Children often have feelings of great loss during a divorce. A young person feels abandoned by the parent who leaves and by the feared loss of their love. This is why it is so important to keep the avenues of communication open between parents and their children during a divorce. Sometimes this is very hard. During a divorce, parents are usually very upset themselves, and find it hard to talk about what is happening.

Lack of self-esteem and no real sense of self-importance also hurts young people. They often feel they don't matter to their parents or to anyone else, for that matter. An attempted suicide is a cry for attention. They want someone to say, "I love you! I don't want you to die!"

Quite often depression is caused by anger turned inward. Instead of expressing it, depressed people keep their anger hidden inside until it starts to affect how they see themselves and the world around them.

One young man who tried to kill himself felt tremendous anger at his father. Bill's father was an alcoholic who beat Bill and his two brothers whenever he had too much to drink. Unable to deal with his father or his home life, Bill drove the family truck into a tree. His two brothers, however, never attempted suicide even though they were growing up in the same family.

What was the difference? Bill's brothers expressed their anger and resentment openly all the time. They might yell and storm out of the house. But Bill was not that kind of person. He kept everything inside. He never tried to communicate any of his emotions, because he felt no one in his family would listen anyway. This feeling of hopelessness slowly made him feel as if he had no importance to anyone at all -- especially himself.

Parental Pressure

Another cause of suicide attempts among young people in this country (as in Japan) is the pressure to succeed. This is often the result of having insecure parents who set impossibly high standards for their kids. Parents who don't feel good about themselves don't want to hear about "bad" things their children do. It makes them feel they haven't done a good job of

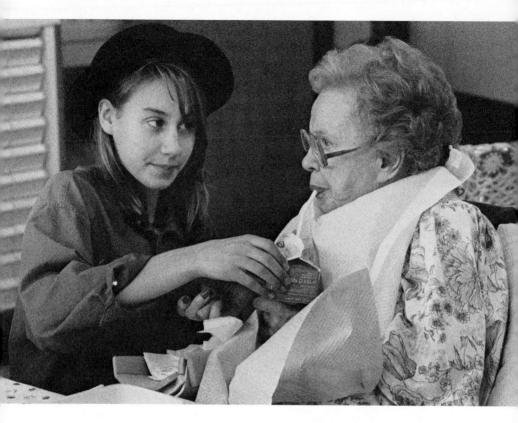

This teenager volunteers at a local nursing home. Sharing and caring for others is an excellent way to get perspective on your own problems.

being parents.

Sexual pressures can also drive young people to try to kill themselves. Puberty is a time of very strong hormonal changes. Young people have adult responses to these physical changes, but they usually aren't allowed to express them in adult ways.

Sometimes young girls who consider suicide are either pregnant or afraid they are pregnant. The fear of discovery—and angering their parents—is so great that it makes them want to take their own lives.

Claire was a 15 year-old who had been sleeping with her boyfriend for a couple of months. She got pregnant, but was terrified of what her parents' reaction would be. She didn't feel she could talk to them, and there was no one else she felt she could talk to. When she told her boyfriend, he became just as frightened and told her he didn't want to see her anymore.

Claire's grades started to fall, and she kept away from her girlfriends, afraid they would find out. She started thinking about killing herself, and began working out the method she would use.

What Claire didn't know was that her mother would, in fact, understand what had happened and try to help her. When Claire's mother guessed her condition, she took her aside and talked with her. Claire didn't try to kill herself after all, but it had been a close call. Other young women don't always have such understanding parents. They think they have no one to turn to and that no one will help them, and as a result their lives are lost. There is help available—they just don't know who or where.

Another situation that can lead to despair for a young person are fears that he or she may be homosexual. Unfortunately, there is still strong social prejudice attached to homosexuality. Some persons would rather take their own lives than live with the difficulties in not being able to conform to their family's or society's expectations.

Sexual abuse can also trigger a suicide attempt. Many young people who have been sexually abused are afraid to tell what happened to them. Sometimes they are threatened with violence by the abuser if they tell. They are also afraid they will be blamed for what happened. Adults often accuse teenagers of having "asked for it." But sexual abuse is a severe trauma. It attacks the basis of a young person's trust in all adults. The abused young person not only has to carry the burden of this "shameful secret," but they also feel betrayed by the very people who were supposed to take care of them.

Several years ago, a boy from New Jersey killed himself because he was sexually molested by a priest during summer camp. He felt no one would believe him if he told. The shame was too much for him to handle alone.

Moving to a new neighborhood and school can trigger a young person's suicide attempt. They feel they don't fit in. They have a hard time making new friends and become very isolated. The great increase in teenage suicides in the last 20 years may be partly due to the many moves families are forced to make because of changing jobs.

In some cases, teenagers feel they are destined to kill themselves because a close family member did. There may be a combination of guilt, revenge, or a strange need to justify the earlier suicide by doing the same thing.

Of course there can always be physical problems such as chemical imbalances in the brain, or other biological reasons that may cause some adolescents to kill themselves. But by and large these are not the most common ones. Emotional abuse or neglect appear to be much stronger factors in teenage suicide.

Adolescence means young people have to re-create themselves almost entirely. They are no longer children. They begin to feel so much adult-sized stress that it's no wonder they get depressed. What they need is assurance that they can reach out to their parents for help. They need to feel loved and wanted, and to be taken seriously.

A combination of many emotional reasons may make a young person try to take his or her life. Suicide is sometimes seen as a foolproof way to solve all of one's problems. Most people, young people included, think about destroying themselves when they believe no one understands and that there is no other way out. Some teenagers have been given everything they could want, but what they really need during difficult times are attention and support.

FOUR UNHAPPY YOUNG PEOPLE

Thirteen-year-old Denise always thought she was fat. Her body had started to change in the sixth grade, and from that time on everyone treated her differently. Boys teased her, and her girlfriends started to shy away from her. Denise was embarrassed by the changes taking place in her body.

She had also always liked sports. But now there were certain days of the month when she was afraid she would have an "accident." She stopped playing field hockey. She stopped swimming. That's when she started gaining weight. At first, Denise said, "The fat was good. I could sort of bury myself in it."

Soon she started to go through times when she wanted to be thin. She would eat, then she would make herself throw up afterwards. This binge-and-vomit cycle is called *bulimia*. Many young women (and some young men) suffer from it.

"Even though I looked thin to other people, I always looked fat to myself. I started taking laxatives all the time," she said. "The laxatives became a good way to lose weight fast.

"Once, before the seventh grade picnic, that was going to be held at the beach, I was so embarrassed by the way I looked in a bathing suit, I took eight laxatives. Believe me, I lost a lot of weight that day.

"My parents never knew I was bulimic, because I always had dinner with them. But then I threw up afterwards. My weight went down to 85 pounds,

Expressing emotions is a healthy way of dealing with your feelings.

and it should be around 110."

But still Denise felt fat.

She disliked herself, and she disliked her body. She had never gotten along well with her mother, and once she reached puberty, things just got worse. Both of her parents were older than most of her friends' parents.

"I always thought my mother liked it better when I was a little girl," Denise confessed. "That way she seemed younger. But when I started to grow up, it was as if I was a public announcement that my mother wasn't as young as she used to be."

It was then that the relationship Denise had with her mother really disintegrated. It added to what was already making her afraid of growing up. She became afraid of the way boys and men would react to her as well. Although she was a very pretty girl, she deliberately set out to make herself ugly.

When high school began, Denise didn't want to go. She was scared of everything. So she took 35 aspirin.

"I just couldn't face any of it. Everything hurt so bad, I didn't care anymore."

Denise's mother found her, and she was taken to the hospital. They pumped her stomach and saved her life, but later Denise tried suicide two more times. On the third try, she took pills and drank a bottle of vodka. This time she succeeded. By the time they found her, it was too late.

Denise was isolated from her parents. She was afraid to start relationships among her peer group. She was very lonely. With no one to talk to, she had no way of working through the fear of her own sexuality. All she could do was make herself so thin that she wouldn't look like a girl anymore. Her fear of growing up took over completely and eventually killed her.

Sandy

Popularity with one's peers in school is extremely important to most teens. Not fitting in often leads to loneliness and depression.

Sandy was 15 years old when her parents moved to a new town a thousand miles away from where she had lived all her life. In her old house Sandy was surrounded by a large, Italian family. Her grandparents lived with them, and her cousins lived two houses down the street. Practically everyone in the neighborhood was related in one way or another.

Sandy's family was strict and old fashioned. She went to parochial school. Her grandmother watched her walk to school from the second story window, and watched for her to come home. There was never a time when Sandy wasn't under someone's watchful eye. But once her parents moved away from the old neighborhood, Sandy felt at a complete loss.

"I went to the public school," she said. "It was real hard for me to make friends. Both my parents were working to pay for the new house. I was doing real bad in school."

Sandy's grandfather used to help her with her homework, but now there was nobody to ask. Her grades started to fall. It wasn't long before everything else started to slide as well.

"My Dad had a liquor cabinet," said Sandy. "I used to come home from school and have some vodka. I'd mix it with orange juice, so it wouldn't be so obvious that I'd been drinking. Then this girl at school gave me some pills. They were supposed to be for cramps."

A few months later, Sandy's grandfather died. She was very upset. She missed him and the whole family. She felt terrible that she hadn't been able to see him again before he died. She wanted to be back in her old town, but that was impossible.

That's when Sandy started taking the pills even when she didn't have cramps. She still wasn't making friends, and was doing even worse in school.

"One day, I failed the midterm. I was so unhappy, I went home and drank the whole bottle of vodka. I didn't even water it down like I usually did so they wouldn't notice."

Unfortunately, what Sandy didn't know was that mixing pills and alcohol was very dangerous. Her mother came home, found Sandy unconscious, and called for help. She was taken to the hospital. Her stomach was pumped.

"The doctor asked me, 'Why did you do it?'

'Do what?' I asked. I didn't know what he was talking about. They all thought I'd tried to kill myself, but that wasn't what I was doing. I was trying to stop the pain, that's all. I thought if I drank a lot, I'd get numb. I'd stop feeling so bad."

The doctors recommended that Sandy be hospitalized.

"It wasn't so bad," she said. "But they weren't too careful. I used to keep the pills they gave me. I hid a whole bunch under my bed. It was my insurance. Nobody ever noticed."

Sandy was having trouble sleeping in the hospital. She'd wake up every night about two o'clock in the morning.

"After about two weeks I just thought, I can't take this anymore. I got up and went into the bathroom. I took all the pills I'd been saving up at once. I felt real good after that. I was peaceful, finally. I went right back to sleep. 'Thank God,' I was thinking. 'Soon this will be over with.'"

Sandy was found unconscious the next morning, and saved once more. She stayed in the hospital for a year, in intensive therapy. It has now been two years since she got out, and she hasn't tried to kill herself again.

After a difficult first year, Sandy started making friends. She began to feel at home in the new school. Her relationship with her mother wasn't much better, but Sandy understood that it wasn't her fault. She now feels accepted by others, and that's one reason she hasn't tried to kill herself again.

"But sometimes I think about it," she says. "I guess it makes me feel better, knowing I can always check out any time I want. I just don't want to so much anymore."

Jimmy

Jimmy was 14 years old when his older brother Bob joined the Marines. Bob was the oldest, and even though they'd been close, Jimmy had always had trouble trying to live up to Bob's example. Bob was good at sports, a natural athlete, good in school, and very popular with girls.

Jimmy, on the other hand, was not very coordinated, just 100 pounds, and did poorly in school. To top it off, Bob was clearly his father's favorite.

"I always had the feeling that it wouldn't have mattered much to Dad and Mom if I'd never been born. Bob was enough for them."

He wasn't popular with his classmates, either. This had never mattered much to Jimmy, because he'd always had Bob to hang around with. Bob was a good older brother.

When Bob went into the Marines, Jimmy was left pretty much alone. Most conversations he had with his parents centered around what Bob was doing, and what a great guy Bob was. Sometimes they harassed Jimmy for not being more like Bob.

Soon Jimmy started feeling like a complete nobody—as if he didn't exist anymore. He only existed in relation to Bob. No Bob, no Jimmy.

Then Bob was killed in an accident. Everyone's world fell apart. Jimmy's parents were crushed. Their grief was noisy and long lasting. Nobody asked Jimmy how he felt about Bob's death, even though he was mourning Bob's loss as much as his parents were. There was no one he felt he could talk to about it. Jimmy's father started drinking a lot. One night he took a walk and never came back. He stood in the middle of the six-lane freeway and was struck and killed by a car.

"He never cared about how I felt," Jimmy said later. "He never cared whether or not I needed a dad. He loved Bob so much, he didn't want to live without him. Having me wasn't good enough. And I was so lonely I couldn't stand the thought of living without Bob, either."

Jimmy had suffered two big losses. First his big brother, the only person he could talk to was gone, and now his father. If his father had cared at all about him, thought Jimmy, he would not have killed himself.

Jimmy took some cyanide from the high school chemistry lab and drank it. He didn't die, but he was very sick for a long time. After a year in therapy, Jimmy now understands something about what happened to him. He knows that just because a parent kills himself doesn't mean you need to do the same thing. But it has been very hard for him. Jimmy's mother took him to live with her family, and in some ways this has helped. Jimmy's grandfather and grandmother, though not easy people to live with, are people who can show affection. Jimmy is getting better, making friends, and doing well in school.

Mary

Mary's parents had divorced when she was only four years old. Mary lived with her mother, who worked long hours. Mary didn't get to see her father very often. He had remarried and started a new family only a year after the divorce.

Dr. Glenn Weimer of Texas is just one of many therapists nationwide who man suicide hotlines. When a person feels nothing but despair, talking with an experienced counselor can mean the difference between life and death.

"Don's new wife didn't like to be reminded that he'd been married before," said Mary's mother. "I guess she sort of influenced how often he saw Mary."

Mary didn't do very well in school because she had an undiagnosed learning disability. Even though she tried very hard to do well, the other kids thought she was stupid. Mary was a loner, although not really by choice.

By the time Mary became a teenager, she had never really managed to develop a friendly relationship with anyone in school.

The short poem "Resume" by 20th-century writer Dorothy Parker takes a light-hearted look at a few good reasons to skip suicide.

Resume

Razors pain you;

Rivers are damp;

Acids stain you;

And drugs cause cramp.

Guns aren't lawful;

Nooses give;

Gas smells awful;

You might as well live.

—Dorothy Parker

"I didn't know she was in trouble," said Mary's mother. "After all, she was never a problem. She never ran with the wrong group, she never talked back, she was just real quiet."

Perhaps Mary's mother should have worried about her grades, but she herself had never done very well in school. She also didn't have time to pay much attention to Mary's schoolwork. And even if she had, she wouldn't have known how to help her. Getting a private tutor was beyond their means.

"If Mary had asked me for help," her mother said, "I would have tried to figure out something. But she never said anything. She just stayed home most of the time and watched a lot of television."

There was no warning as far as Mary's mother was concerned. One afternoon when she got home from work, she found Mary in the bathtub with deeply slashed wrists. She called 911, but it was too late. Mary was already dead when help arrived.

All four young people had many things in common. Each was lonely. Each felt—rightly or wrongly—that they had no one they could talk to. The lines of communication had broken down completely within their families.

In every case the situation faced by the boy or girl was bad, but not impossible. Denise, Sandy, Jimmy and Mary didn't know that there were much easier and better ways to deal with their despair. They also didn't know that their despair was only temporary.

Even though it didn't seem to their families that there were any warning signs, in fact there were. Unfortunately, nobody recognized them. It is important for everyone to understand the problems that young people face during adolescence. Teachers, parents and the clergy should be trained to recognize signs of isolation and depression.

Sometimes all it takes to help a young person in distress are a few words, or some recognition on the part of people who live and work with them. Those few words can mean the difference between saving a life and letting one go tragically.

FIVE

LEARN THE WARNING SIGNS

Teenagers who reach the point where they are thinking of suicide almost always send out very clear warning signals. They are cries for help. Some clues are not always understood, but out of every ten young people who plan to kill themselves, eight will give definite signals beforehand. These warning signs are called *prodromal clues,* and they are the key to preventing a potential suicide.

Often the young person will talk about suicide or send some other kind of verbal clue. Some are very direct, such as "I can't stand this much longer," "Everyone would be happier without me," or "Nobody cares what I do."

Sometimes the remarks are in the form of questions such as, "How do guns work?" or "Just what do you have to do to leave your body to science?" There are other instances when a young person will ask about suicide, but make it sound like they're talking about a friend. It is important to pay attention if you hear someone say it. Research shows that most young people who kill themselves have said similar things shortly before they actually act.

Three quarters of potential suicides have also started having some kind of physical problem—usually within the preceding four months. They may suffer from stomachaches, headaches, vision problems, or something else that sends them to a doctor. They can also have sleeping problems. They may either sleep a lot more than usual or wake up periodically during the night. Sleeping a lot is an easy way of escaping problems. Some teenagers also report an increase in nightmares.

Persistent warning signs in children and young

A good friend is a good listener. Paying attention when someone talks or jokes about suicide is important—they may be serious about taking their own life.

adults can also include a sudden personality change, anxiety, depression, anorexia, and frequent outbursts of bad temper. A severe change in eating habits may also signal a suicidal state. Increased eating, drinking, smoking, or consuming sweets in large amounts are signs of problems. Refusing to eat or losing lots of weight could also be a sign.

As young people get closer to making their decision, they often do things that look like they are making final arrangements. They may give away some of their most prized possessions.

Young people often go out of their way to break

the rules. They may not be so out of control that they do things that are illegal, but their rebellion may get them into a great deal more trouble than usual.

For example, a 13-year-old boy whose parents were in the middle of a divorce asked a friend to make him a pipe bomb. The friend sold him what amounted to half a stick of dynamite with a very short fuse. This bomb was not well made, and it could have easily blown up if his mother hadn't found it and called the police. Since the boy did not hide it particularly well, it can be assumed that he wanted someone to find it and realize he was having problems.

Teachers can often detect serious trouble in the creative writing of their students. There are often clues in poems or short stories that dwell on death. An increased interest in music and art that talks about death, murder, or suicide should also be noticed. A teacher can always ask the young person to talk about their story to learn what, if anything, is going on under the surface. Writing is an invitation to talk. More times than not, a troubled teenager will open up to someone if given half a chance.

Any of the following signs, seen together with some of the more basic underlying ones, should be taken very seriously.

If a young person seems to be too shy or have very few friends, they may in fact have serious problems. Some adolescents seem to want to drive other young people away from them by acting hostile, idiotic, or stupid. This can be just another way of isolating themselves. For example, a perfectly bright and interesting young person may go to extremes to keep others from liking him or her. Acting up in school in such a way that makes teachers as well as students want to avoid this student has the exact same effect as simply withdrawing on their own. It only serves to reinforce the negative feelings the student already has about their self image.

If someone has little or no feelings of self worth, they don't know how to accept the friendly gestures of people around them. They are almost saying, "No one could possibly like me. If someone seems to, they've got to be crazy, so therefore I don't like them."

A young person who is suicidal often stops being interested in his or her personal appearance. They stop taking care of personal hygiene, they cut classes, or get involved with drugs and alcohol. They stop showing any interest in the future.

Low self-esteem makes it very hard for adolescents to reach out. They don't have a solid sense of who they are or what will become of them. They have lots of questions, but very few answers.

Many parents of young people who have either tried or succeeded in committing suicide will think back and remember the warning signals their children sent. But the lack of communication between these parents and their children made it easy for them to ignore these warnings. Facing the fact that your child is desperately unhappy is very difficult for most parents to do. If their child is miserable, does that make them bad parents? Of course not. Good parents can have suicidal children, too.

Because of the way society thinks about and treats suicide, there is no easy way to talk about it. But talking about it is what must be done to prevent it from happening.

SIX

PREVENTION: WHAT TO DO

The most important thing to remember about preventing suicide is this: do something! Take some action.

If you think someone is going to commit suicide, or if you feel like committing suicide, don't ignore it. Suicide is a major cause of death that has to be recognized and treated, just like other deadly problems. Researchers work tirelessly to find a cure for cancer. Parents try to stop drunk driving. Why should suicide be treated any differently? After all, most young people have perfect health and many years ahead of them. For such a large number to die needlessly is senseless.

Talking about it really does help. Most reasons young people have for killing themselves can be solved through communication and proper treatment.

What often appears to be an intolerable situation is usually only temporary. Having no friends can be solved. Feeling unwanted or unloved can be solved. Not doing well in school isn't the end of the world.

A young person very often finds out after an attempted suicide that his or her parents are indeed supportive. It wasn't necessary to take such self destructive action to get their attention.

It is also important to define a young person's priorities. If he or she is feeling tremendous pressure to succeed, just discussing it often helps them figure out what they really want and the best way to go about getting it. Young people should learn to recognize what is best for them, and pay less attention to what other people want or expect. Since the aim of life is to be happy, it naturally follows that doing things that make you happy with yourself is the only way to live. Killing yourself won't make you

Why They Do It

The most frequent reasons that teenagers give therapists for wanting to die are the following:

• They want to get some relief for an intolerable state of mind.

• They want to escape from an impossible situation, even for just a while.

• They want to make people around them understand just how desperate they feel.

• They want to get back at people who have hurt or upset them. They also want to make them feel sorry.

• They want to use the suicide attempt as a way to make someone change their mind about something.

• They want to show someone how very much they love them.

• They want to find out if someone really loves them or not.

• They are crying out for help.

happy, it will simply make you dead.

If you know someone who is a potential suicide, never keep it a secret. Try to talk to that person, or make sure an adult knows about it. Talk to your own parents. Talk to a teacher or member of the clergy. Or call a suicide prevention program or hotline.

Sometimes teenagers don't tell when a friend is talking about suicide because they have been sworn to secrecy. But why would a friend be angry at you for keeping them alive? What they wanted in the first place was knowing that someone, somewhere, loved and cared about them. It is possible that the person will be angry at first, but they'll understand that you disclosed the secret to save them. Saving a person from committing suicide is one of the most important ways to show you care about them and what happens to them.

Another very important thing to remember is to follow up on the person. Just because someone stops talking about suicide for a while doesn't mean they are in the clear. Potential suicides often seem to cheer up a great deal for no apparent reason, and everyone around them thinks it is a sign that they have gotten over their depression.

Unfortunately, many times it doesn't mean that at all. Instead it means that after much thought, they made up their mind. After having made their decision, they are relaxed and happy because they know they are about to do something that will end their pain and depression forever.

Learning About Suicide

Education may be one of the single most important means of suicide prevention. There needs to be more specific programs in schools and churches that talk with young people about the stresses they face and how to deal with them. The taboo surrounding the subject of suicide must be lifted. Many people feel that talking about suicide will only encourage it, but the exact opposite seems to be true. The notion that talking about suicide puts the idea into a young person's mind is false. If someone wants to commit suicide, talking about it helps discourage them. If they don't want to commit suicide they don't feel more inclined to do so simply because they heard or read about it.

Helping young people recognize that they have power over their own lives, power to make good things happen to them and not just bad things, is the most important part of these information programs.

A good suicide prevention program would help all teenagers recognize the symptoms of depression, and what teenagers can expect to happen while they are still growing up.

Society's obsession with what is "normal" needs to be addressed too. Not being in step with your peers is a common cause of depression in young people. Yet it is very difficult for anyone to define "normal"—even psychologists argue about it. A young person with very rigid ideas about what is "normal" needs to see that there is a lot of leeway in life, and that there is room for everyone.

Family counseling is an excellent way to curb the emotional problems that can lead to suicide.

For More Information

If you or a friend need help with a problem that seems overwhelming, and you feel you cannot talk with your parents, try talking with an adult you can trust. It may be a favorite teacher, a school guidance counselor, a coach of your after school athletic team, or maybe your boss (if you have a part-time job).

If there is no one you know that you want to talk to, look in your local phone directory for some groups that offer suicide counseling. These can include city, county or state agencies, or private, non-profit counseling centers. Ask the operator for assistance if you can't find a listing that sounds right. But don't be afraid to call and ask.

If you can't think of who to call, here are two numbers to call toll free:

The Humanistic Mental Health Foundation
1 (800) 777-5421

Suicide Intervention 24-Hour Hotline
1 (800) 444-9999

Glossary

ADOLESCENCE. A period between childhood and adulthood when males and females alike go through sexual maturity; puberty.

ANOREXIA. A condition characterized by complete loss of appetite and a corresponding weight loss that can be life-threatening.

AUTOCIDE. A term coined to indicate that a fatal car accident was intended as a way of committing suicide.

BULIMIA. A disorder where a person eats and then vomits everything consumed. It is often linked to anorexia.

EXTENDED FAMILY. A family group where the relatives all live in very close proximity to each other.

HARA KIRI. An ancient form of suicide practiced in Japan as a way of erasing disgrace.

HOMICIDE. The deliberate killing of another human being.

KAMIKAZE PILOTS. Japanese World War II flyers who killed themselves by flying their planes into enemy warships. This death was considered honorable.

MARTYR. A person who dies on purpose for a political or religious cause.

PRODROMAL CLUES. Warning signals of potential suicidal behavior.

PUBERTY. The stage in growth where a person becomes physiologically capable of sexual reproduction.

SUICIDE. The act of intentionally killing oneself.

Bibliography

Alvarez, A. *The Savage God: A Study of Suicide*.
Random House, 1972

Crow, Gary A. & Letha I. *Crisis Intervention and
Suicide Prevention: Working with Children and
Adolescents*. Charles C. Thomas, Publisher, 1987

Davis, Patricia A. *Suicidal Adolescents*. Charles C.
Thomas Publisher, 1983

Gardner, Sandra. *Teenage Suicide*. Julian Messner, 1985

Hawton, Keith. *Suicide and Attempted Suicide Among
Children and Adolescents*. Sage Publications,
Inc., 1986

Heillig, Roma J. *Adolescent Suicidal Behavior*. UMI
Reserach Press, 1980, 1983

Parker, A. Morgan. *Suicide Among Young Adults*.
Exposition Press, 1974

Schneidman, Edwin S. *Clues To Suicide*. McGraw Hill
Book Company, 1957

Index

Photo Credits